Come Out with Your Hands Up

The Joy of Surrendering on God's Terms

Come Out with Your Hands Up

The Joy of Surrendering on God's Terms

Kimberley McDaniel

Wasteland Press
Louisville, KY

Wasteland Press
Louisville, KY USA
www.wastelandpress.com

Come Out with Your Hands Up
By Kimberley McDaniel

Copyright © 2003 Kimberley McDaniel

First Printing - July, 2003

ISBN: 0-9742342-6-5

Unless otherwise indicated, all Scripture references are taken from the King James Version of the Holy Bible.

Printed In U.S.A.

§§§

This Book Belongs
to

_____

who dares you to
Come Out with Your Hands Up!

§§§

*This book is lovingly dedicated
to my wonderful husband, Corvelli,
who provides steadfast support in my
every endeavor, and to my 3 sweeties,
Victoria, Jesse, and Kennedy.
The love of my family is astounding and
I know that God has blessed me
beyond measure.*

Dear Esteemed Reader,

Imagine being given an opportunity to start your life all over again. Your physical body would stay the same, but your mind and spirit would be elevated to a height of tremendous wisdom and understanding. This new life would offer many benefits to you, the most important being a personal consultant who would be at your disposal 24 hours a day. Let me share some of the consultant's character traits with you, before you decide whether or not you want him working for you, with you, and through you:

- He has your best interest at heart;
- He possesses the winning plan for your life;
- He will fight all of your battles for you;
- He will teach you how to persevere.

Your only obligation is to this advisor is to exercise an attitude of complete trust, obedience, and gratitude. The best aspect about this relationship is that your mentor has wisdom, power, and mercy at his disposal. He can turn situations around in the blink of an eye. He can make your enemies bless you and expose those who are trying to curse you. He can exchange your weakness for his strength, your fear for his faith, and your worry for his peace. And these characteristics that he possesses are foundationally strong and sincere to the core. His peace will not be moved; his faith will not waiver; and his strength cannot be diluted.

Are you interested in meeting him? If you had a friend like that on your side, how likely would your victories be? Would you have greater success in your home, on your job, and in your relationships? Would you be able to walk taller and with more confidence, knowing in advance that the victory is yours? This consultant is putting out a call to arms, summoning all persons who want to live their life with purpose and on purpose by following His expertise. That means that it is time to stop playing life and to embrace it for what it is by not wasting our time majoring on the minors and minoring on the majors. It is time for a total recall - we need to reassess our "who" instead of busying ourselves with our "what."

We are so preoccupied with labels that we sometimes lose sight of the real success stories. This book is going to help you strip away the labels and look into your soul. Who are you? It will help you to look at your true motives, which are your driving actions which reveal your inner most person. We will not be dealing with Mother, Pastor, Doctor, Teacher, but rather, Woman of Integrity, Man of Honor, Child of Peace. Once these qualities are recognized and reassured in your spirit, then we can hone them and use them as markers along your success route. The proverbial ladder of success is a relative term. Those who climb ladders of integrity, righteousness, and mercy, will have much more to rely on as they go through various dramatic events in their life time. Labels come and they go, but your own self-identity, perception, and awareness, are an important parts of what will help you endure. Knowing that God has deemed you so worthy that He has designed a tailor made plan for your life - this information can sustain you during even the toughest times. The realization that you matter to Him will help you keep all matters in perspective.

His plans and desires for you are so marvelous that if He were to show you the end result, you would shake your head in awe, disbelief, and amazement. He will not drag you along the road to success, but He will drive you. He wants so much for you, that He has sent a personal assistant to ensure your success. This person comes highly recommended and has never failed a client. He wants only the best for you, not because you deserve it, but because He loves you that much. Your best, as per His definition, may not always seem like a choice you would make, but that's part of the beauty of this relationship.

You can trust Him...

Behold, I stand at the door and knock;
if any man hear my voice,
and open the door,
I will come in to him,
and will sup with him,
and he with me.

Revelation 3:20

You Have the Right
to Remain Silent

If you were arrested for being a Christian, would there be enough evidence to convict you? God has sent a special One Man Task Force to seek you out. This Person has committed to laying His life on the line for you. When He knocks on the door of your heart, it is imperative that you welcome Him in. Feel free to let your guard down and let Him see you just as you are. You do not have to put on makeup or comb your hair before answering the door. He has already seen you at your worse and He loves you anyway. You do not have to clean yourself up - He will take it from here. The journey is just beginning and you are about to embark on a trip that will shake you at your very foundation. You are about to start living the life that He has prepared for you - it is time to meet your destiny. Your destiny is not a place; it is a Person - His name is Jesus, and He encompasses everything you need to excel. If you even thought you were living before, know that the best is yet to come.

Now when you let Him in, understand that He is going to take you into His custody. Your role is to surrender. You must come out with your hands up. This is a sign of good faith, a way to show Him your hands are empty and that you are not holding on to any devices from your past life that would represent a conflict with His plans for you. You may not see yourself as God's adversary, but in reality, we all have chosen one of two sides. You are either for God or against Him. Someone told me of a parable that depicted God and Satan at the end of time, dividing the souls of all mankind. In this large waiting area, there were apparently two groups of people, divided by a fence. Some individuals were on God's side, and they clearly went with Him.

Another group, on the other side of the fence, joined Satan's eternal family. Finally, there was a great multitude of people, who was sitting on the fence - Satan demanded they come with him. They said, "Wait a minute, we have not chosen to be on your side - we are sitting squarely on the fence." Satan answered in a confident manner, "I know; I own the fence."

Upon opening the door and inviting Christ into our heart, we must greet Him with a sincere attitude of surrender. We are basically admitting that we cannot fulfill our purpose without Him as the Center of our life. By inviting Christ into our life, we are seeking reconciliation - we want to be made one with Christ. As sinners, before we accept Him as our personal savior, the sin in our life is a gulf between us and God. We cannot bridge that gap - it is too wide, too deep and too dirty. The good news is that God knew this, so He sent His Son, Jesus to reconcile us to Him. When He was nailed to the cross on Calvary, 2,000 years ago, He took on the sins of the world, in a general sense. And He took on your sins and my sins, in a very personal sense. That is why He is hailed as the Savior of the world as well as a Personal Savior. Our only responsibility is to open the door and let Him in. Some of us want to interrogate Him, while He is still on the porch. We have a laundry list of questions based on contingencies. Questions like, "If I let you in, will I have to give up _____?" "What if I discover this Christian life is too hard - will I be able to go back home?" These are just a couple of examples that point to the main problem with this line of reasoning. God loves us unconditionally and is willing to accept us, just as we are.

~~~~~~

You are either for God
or against Him - there
is no middle ground..

~~~~~~

We must learn to trust Him early on in the relationship or we will never go beyond our own expectations. But upon your initial introduction, when He is looking directly at your heart, what should you do and say? Hindsight being 20/20, I can say today, that I would plead the fifth.

I would ask for the right to remain silent and reflective. Jesus is my example - when He was declared guilty of blasphemy before the highest courts of His day, He invoked His rights. Isaiah 53:7 tells us that "He was oppressed and afflicted, yet He opened not His mouth: he is brought as a lamb to the slaughter, and as a sheep before her shearer is dumb, so He openeth not His mouth." In all His righteousness, purity, perfection and holiness, He chose silence. How much more can we say in our sad state of unrighteousness, filth and depravity? Ecclesiastes, one of the great books of wisdom, tells us that there is a time to speak and there is a time for silence.

The only reason I do not recommend the former option, first, is because it is our natural tendency to rationalize, justify, make excuses, and place blame. Instead of telling God how sorry we are, we would be likely to tell Him about how much we have been victimized and eventually end up pointing the finger at Him. Just ask Adam and Eve, the first humans to try to bank on extenuating circumstances. When God confronted them, Adam said it was Eve's fault and Eve quickly blamed it on the serpent. Some things change and some things stay the same.

After your time of silence and reflection, however brief it may be, the moment will come for accountability and confession. As you measure your next words, choose them wisely, keeping in mind that the goal is quality, not quantity. If you find that you are compelled to say more than, "I surrender," look at the key components below, for a textbook heart transplant:

1) Confess to God that you are a sinner (Romans 3:23)
2) Believe on Jesus in your heart - that He set aside His deity

to come here in the flesh to pay the price for your sins
(Romans 10:9 and Philippians 2:5-8)
3) Ask God to forgive you and commit your new life to Him
(2 Corinthians 5:17)

These steps all boil down to two words: **I surrender**.

Again, it is the quality of your utterance that matters most. If you were to step back and look at the situation from a bigger picture, what else is there to say, really, that would explain away any of your behavior or decisions made up to this point, regarding not accepting Him in your life?

We recently attended a couple of family weddings and my 8 year old asked about the significance of the location of the wedding ring on the left hand. I told him that tradition says that the ring finger follows the vena amoris, the vein of love, which is connected directly to the heart. Just like many traditions, the veracity of the origination is not readily verifiable. I can say with surety, however, that there is a direct connection between the heart and the mouth.

> Let the words of my mouth,
> and the meditations of my heart,
> be acceptable in thy sight...
>
> Psalm 19:14

Out of the abundance of the heart, the mouth speaketh.
> Matthew 12:34

The next logical question would be - what exactly is in your heart, in an abundant quality, that would overflow into your conversation? Jeremiah helps us by leaving no room for speculation:

The heart is deceitful above all things
and desperately wicked: who can know it.

Jeremiah 17:9

The Hebrew translation of the word for **deceitful**, is *aqob* - in our present day language, this means fraudulent, crooked, or polluted. I was familiar with this passage and thought I already knew what wicked meant. After all, how many different ways could one refer to evil? After some research, I found that Jeremiah was using the Hebrew word, *anash*, which translated, means, frail, pitiful, and incurable. God sees us as insufferably lost, in a maze, with no way out.

I imagine God looks at us sometimes and just shakes His head in pity and dismay. Imagine a parent who has seen the great potential of his son, throughout his entire academic life, and then when it's time for him to make his mark on the world, he chooses to hang out on the street corners and watch the world go by. The parent would have to say, "What is going on with you - why don't you see what I see!" God is similar to the degree that He is our Father; He knows our potential; and He knows all the right choices we ought to be making. And though we disappoint Him, He does not abandon us. He knows that we cannot save ourselves.

In spite of the outward sin - disrespect of self or others, drug abuse, adultery, lying, jealousy, dishonesty, murder, addiction, etcetera - these are all symptomatic of a deeper, chronic problem. At the root of your soul, the very core of your being, lies the switch that compels you to pick a sin, any sin. That root is your heart condition - that feeble minded heart of yours that is the command center of your life.

It is from the abundance of this distorted and dysfunctional footing, that we dare to address the holy and living God. No, I think that this would be the time to hold our peace in His presence. The Spirit of God is inexplicably merciful and one sign of that is the fact that He has given us a free will. He is not going to force us to love Him nor demand we present to Him a lengthy defense to explain our behavior. I would walk in His grace and just come out with my hands up in a posture of surrender and invoke my right to remain silent, as the tears of thankfulness flowed down my cheeks.

You can trust Him;
Just Him...

Anything You Say
Can Be Used Against You...

You are now in His custody and you are going over in your mind exactly what just happened. There is also a tendency to reflect over your life and wonder how you got out alive. It is at this point that you start to have your first glimpses of His mercy. During some parts of your stroll down memory lane, you will undoubtedly run across The Accuser. That is another nickname for Satan. As you grow in your Christian walk, you will get to see many sides of him - all bad. His first mission is to keep you away from God. He wants you to have sufficient pride in your spirit that will keep you from admitting that you need Christ as your Redeemer. Once you disappoint him by accepting the invitation to join God's family, he will then focus on stunting your growth so as to minimize your opportunity to walk in God's grace and plan for your life.

The crippling side effect of stunting your growth is the impact that your bipolar Christian testimony will have on your audience - you know these people as friends, family, co-workers, passersby, etc. If he can get you to lead them far enough down the path of confusion whereby they want no part of what you've got, then he has made a two for one coup. The enemy has many ploys; one of his key strategies is conspiratorial in nature. He wants to partner with you and have you accuse yourself. If he trains you well enough, he can leave the scene and trust that you will pick up and continue where he left off.

In the following simple illustration, I want to lay out a realistic course of events that could enter the life of a new (or even a seasoned) Christian. Let's say for example, before Christ, you did not value your body or self-worth and had a tendency to look for love in all the wrong places. Now that you are in Christ, you realize that God has created you for much greater purposes and you want to turn your back on that lifestyle. So Satan, who knows your weakness, because he has seen your pattern of behavior, helps to arrange a particular situation where you are confronted with some tempting companionship, aimed at leading you down the wrong path. And here you are, newly sanctified, yet still weak in the knees.

Your next moments are crucial. Your heart and mind will speak and your hands and feet will follow. What you say to yourself in these quiet, pre-decision moments, will determine what He will say to you at a later time when He shall have your undivided attention. At that time you will say either, "I'm glad I didn't," or "I sure wish I hadn't."

Let's see how this internal 3 way conversation could play out...

Your Flesh	**Satan**
He (or she) sure looks good; and I heard things aren't going great at home...	Hey, you are two consenting adults - everybody's doing it; You know he is a Christian too - God must have set this up, after all, He created you and the needs you are trying to deny...

Your Spirit
God will not put more on me than I can bear;

The world's standards are not my standards
- a friend of the world is an enemy of God;

I can be holy, because God is holy;

I am fleeing my youthful lusts and am choosing

to follow righteousness, faith, charity, and peace
with them that call on the Lord with a pure heart;

I am blessed when I endure temptation; I shall
receive the crown of life .

When I was a child, I spoke as a child, I understood
as a child, I thought as a child: but when I became
a man (or woman), I put away childish things .

This is just one way the scenario could play itself out.
The examples used in this three way conversation are not unique
to this instance. Satan will try to accuse you whenever he can find
a way in and these attacks may happen several times a day. He
will also not hesitate to initiate conversations - a lot of times, he
just wants to see if you will take the bait. He will use frontal
assaults, ambushes, deceptions and bold lies, all in an attempt to
entrap you. And as you grow in your wisdom and Christian
maturity, his strategy may be to decrease the number of attacks,
because he sees you are not as gullible as you once were. Though
he may lessen the amount, he alters the style - instead of head on
assaults, his methods may become more subtle in nature. Like a
scorned lover, he is relentless in his pursuit. His motto is, the
bigger they are, the harder they fall. If he can be more successful
at blind siding you when you have hundreds of people under your
authority or influence, then he counts that as an even bigger
victory.

In the above scenario, I intentionally used many passages
of scripture for your spirit to access during this battle of words.
You have to immerse yourself in good words, mind altering
words, life changing words. Before you were saved, Satan and
your flesh were the dominant players in your decision making
process and you were consistently bombarded with wrong
choices. Your spirit didn't have an opinion - it was dead. Many
people lean heavily on their conscience as their moral compass,
but that, by itself, has no definite truth. God's truth is the only one
that withstands all trends and other tests of time. Wrapped all in

and around His Truth are thousands of promises for you and me. The Holy Bible is God's love letter to His children. There is nothing in it that you cannot have access to. He encourages us in Isaiah 55:11:

> So shall my word be that goeth forth
> out of my mouth; it shall not return
> unto me void, but it shall accomplish
> that which I please, and it shall prosper
> in the thing whereto I sent it.

Now, as you remind yourself that He made you in His own image, understand that He has put some power in your mouth as well. You have the power to build or the power to destroy. You will have a myriad of moments throughout the day to use your tongue as a weapon of warfare or a tool of peace. The power of the spoken word carries more weight than one could ever imagine.

Sticks and stones may break your bones, but words can kill you. Words will set a person on a one way course, a slow painful increasingly erosive death. The target is the spirit. When your spirit is minimized and constantly attacked, then your very being is at stake. The odd thing about these tactics is that most of the time, they are not truth-based. Inaccurate perception is often the main culprit. Some examples may include childhood taunts or a teacher who may have questioned your potential or even the comments of a passerby might put you in spin cycle, e.g. "When are you due?" and you are not even pregnant. Hurtful comments like these can eat away at our self-confidence for years into the future and they can even affect how we deal with the next generation. This is an inheritance that stings and robs the recipients of their own chance to start with a clean slate. You may have seen it in the way some children are treated - "We never did well in school, so we aren't expecting you to be an 'A' student - we just want you to do your best."

Even more important than what others say to us, is what

we say to ourselves. Everything from, "I've never been good with numbers," to "I always seem to draw the wrong type of man," to "I don't think I'll make a good _____ " (you fill in the blank) - these all have a lasting impact. Look at what Matthew 12:36-37 has to say about the power of the spoken word:

> Every idle word that men shall speak,
> they shall give an account thereof
> in the day of judgment.
> For by thy words thou shalt be justified
> and by thy words thou shalt be condemned.

Let's take a look at Matthew's intentions when he penned these words. The Greek translation of idle, is, argos, which means: unemployed, useless, or barren. In this sense of the definition of idleness, the type of words or conversations that come to mind are those that are offensive to others - those words which assassinate the character and reputation of someone, usually not within hearing distance. Often people will say they refrain from gossip and slander - but without realizing it, they are still tearing down their own character when they inundate themselves with negative thoughts, doubts and criticisms.

Because our inner thoughts fester like wounds, it is only a matter of time before that which is on the inside, explodes on the outside. Over time, those same thoughts lead to an eruption and anyone within range of the explosion will be victimized by the manifested pain. From the outside looking in, all the onlookers scratch their head and wonder, "Where did that come from? I thought everything was fine." In all the intricate, complex designs and physical gifts God has planted in us, He has not given us the ability to read minds. This self talk is the only thing that we can hold as truly private. It is a miraculous gift that we can use in our favor, to build ourselves up, to speak forgiveness into our spirit, or to coach ourselves into greater levels of discipline. Or we can use the converse side and tear ourselves down, mull over the faults of others, or contemplate various strategies of revenge. Words, as they dance through our minds, before they even make it out of our mouths, are packed with power.

One of the popular phrases for the computer information age is "garbage in, garbage out." This expression is even more appropriate when understanding our own emotional development. If a profane, decaying, demented idea comes your way, you have the authority to deny its entry into your mind. It needs your permission to come right in and make itself at home. One of my favorite little poems is by Charles Fletcher Lumis. He puts it this way:

I am bigger than anything that can happen to me.
All these things, sorrow, misfortune,
and suffering, are outside my door.

I am in the house and I have the key.

I am not suggesting that all pain is unavoidable. What I am saying is the only event we can control, is our reaction to outside events. Our first line of defense is seated in our mind and is controlled by our thoughts. I discussed earlier the direct connection between our heart and mouth. That which is in our heart becomes fodder for our thought process. We are emotional creatures who are affected from the outside in. It sometimes seems like the age old question of which came first, the chicken or the egg. But if we did an accurate accounting of our past, we would realize the self-doubt did not appear out of thin air. Someone along your path brought into your arena of choices, the option for you to select weakness or fear in a certain area. your area of weakness at least once. Maybe immediately or over time, you invested into the belief that you were below par in that particular area.

One sign of maturity is realizing that we all have areas of strengths and weaknesses. The unfairness of Satan's attacks is that he often goes for the jugular well before we are mature enough to appreciate the balance of our total personality. The outcome can actually become a life time struggle of self-doubt and even self-hatred. Those seeds placed in our hearts can take root and choke the good fruit that we are truly designed to produce. The cycle thus becomes:

WE GET EXTERNAL IDEAS ===>>
     PLATFORM OF OUR HEART ===>>
          THOUGHTS ===>>
               WORDS & ACTIONS===>>
                    HABITS or LIFESTYLE ===>>

WE PLANT IDEAS...

As you can see, the heart is so vulnerable and accessible to the external environment. We are told in Proverbs to guard our heart with all diligence - it is the most precious possession we own. Once a foothold gets established in there, it is almost as simple as a connect the dots scenario from that point on. Proverbs 23:7 reminds us that "as a man thinketh in his heart, so is he." If we can effectively guard our heart, we are positioning ourselves for victory. Even though the heart is located in the second stage of the process, that is the first part that we can control. The mechanics of controlling our heart is to simply work from a two pronged attack. Purpose what ideas we want to pour into our mind and intentionally think on ideas that will grow you up and move you on to higher levels. On a recent birthday my mother gave me a pin that coined a modern day colloquialism. The bold, colorful pin says, "Whatever!" On the accompanying card, the elaboration reads:

> Whatever is true,
> whatever is noble,
> whatever is right,
> whatever is pure,
> whatever is admirable,
> whatever is honorable...
> think about these things.
>   - Philippians 4:8

This is what we have in our arsenal. I am applying military terminology to our circumstances because we are at war. It is a constant spiritual battle, and everything you do or fail to do moves you closer to God or further away from Him. Our best defense is a hearty offense, so as we intentionally place thoughts of productivity into our mind, our chances for victory are increased. Whatever is seeded into our brain and heart will take root, then sprout, and demand to be harvested. These thoughts will break through the surface and look for a place to land. Here is where we affect others as we plant into their spirits.

~~~~~~

Our best defense against his lies?
An aggressive offense!

~~~~~~

When I was stationed with an Army Aviation Brigade I was fortunate enough to learn a lot about helicopters. I was able to see the versatility of our helicopters when compared to airplanes. The ability to land a plane always demanded an airstrip. Our pilots didn't need much room to land, and they could do it immediately and practically in any location, if necessary. I find that our spoken words are sometimes like helicopters. We don't always use landing strips for our conversation - you know, taking into consideration how the intended recipient will feel upon hearing our sentiments and then taking care to conduct a gentle landing. No, we sometimes tend to speak whatever is on our mind - we don't need a lot of room or provocation. Our words sometimes land wherever they please. They have even been known to make crash landings, destroying everything in sight. And so the cycle continues. You get to be the judge of the type of thoughts you let into your space as well as the types of seeds that you sow into the minds and hearts of others.

Once you control the heart and mind, the mouth will follow. The Bible makes the connection clear in several areas - here are but a few:

> They speak vanity everyone with his neighbor:
> with flattering lips and a double heart do they
> speak. The Lord shall cut off all flattering lips,
> and the tongue that speaketh proud things.
>
> Psalm 12:2-3

> Let your speech be always with grace,
> Seasoned with salt, that ye may know
> how ye ought to answer every man.
>
> Colossians 4:6

> Be not rash with thy mouth,
> and let not thine heart be hasty to utter any thing
> before God: for God is in heaven and thou upon
> earth: therefore let thy words be few.
>
> Ecclesiastes 5:2

Looking at the total picture, we can see that we have a tri-fold responsibility. We must place a sentry at our hearts, not allowing or encouraging destructive ideas to enter. If a negative thought does slip past the gates, we must attack it with due diligence so that it does not take root. The success of this tactic will ensure victory in the third area - how we talk to ourselves and to others. We must purpose to speak words of love, healing, and encouragement, and forgiveness into every relationship of which we are a part. The God we serve, who personifies prosperity, growth, abundance and fruitfulness, would have it no other way - after all, He did create us in His image.

You can trust Him;
Just Him.
Can He trust you...

You Have the Right
to an Attorney

...If you cannot afford an attorney, one will be provided for you. In the modern day judicial system we see all types of represen-tation in the court room - everything from public defendants to pro bono cases to lawyers who charge top dollar. They all have one goal in common: to have their clients set free. Some counselors know their defendant is guilty and their goal is to either plead them out or see that they serve a minimal sentence. In all my years of watching court TV - real life or fictional, I have yet to see a lawyer say, "Yes, my client is guilty of committing heinous crimes and yes he deserves the death penalty, but I will sit in the chair, in his place, and take the needle." That will never happen. Or will it? As a matter of fact, it has already happened.

Jesus was sent here, by His Father, to right your wrongs. Someone had to pay the price - In the 6th chapter of the book of John, the author tells us that the wages (what we owe) of sin is death, but the (free) gift of God is eternal life. What exactly was Jesus' role? Well, a price had to be paid and we could not pay it - we do not have enough in our account to cover the charge. Jesus could have come in a condemning fashion, berating us, threatening us, and forcing us to pay off at least some of our debt. That is what our finite mind would describe as both a reasonable and fair option. The truth of the matter is that there is nothing we can do, in and of ourselves, to work towards our own salvation. His foreknowledge is so revealing - He says in Ephesians that He set it up that way so man would not be in a position to boast. We cannot deny our tendency to beat our proverbial chest, when we accomplish a major feat. And what is greater than positioning ourselves to enter the gates of heaven?

How much louder would we boast if we earned our way to our Father's side? And we won't even discuss looking down at others - you know, that, "If I can do it, why can't you," syndrome. The good news is that we are not on any type of payment plan, nor does He expect matching funds from us. He didn't come to challenge us; He came to change us. John 3:17 tells us:

> For God sent not his Son into the world
> to condemn the world; but that the world
> through Him might be saved.

You may say, what wrongs, what horrible crimes have I committed? I am neither the moral nor spiritual police but I will inform you that God says that all have sinned and come short of the glory of God (Romans 3:23). He goes on to tell us in 1 John that if we say we have no sin, we are lying. What does this most atrocious offense look like, this thing that would actually keep us out of heaven and more importantly, eternally separated from God? This is a legitimate question because some of us have been sinning so long that it has become our norm, and nothing seems out of place. A simple explanation was shared with me regarding the understanding of sin.

God does not examine the fruit; He looks at the root.

Sitting in the middle of sIn is "I". When you live your life in a self-centered fashion, you are putting all your chips on your own abilities. You are saying, I am who I am, what I am, and where I am, because of me, myself, and I. You are worshiping the wrong trinity. Some people do not spend time focused on themselves, but rather pour themselves into other people and causes. From the world's perspective, they are not self-centered, but greatly charitable in their efforts. How can we imagine that their heart is not in the right place - look at their abundance of good works. God does not examine the   fruit; He looks at the root. If people are giving and God is not the recognized source of their initiated action, then they are sharing for the wrong reasons.

God is a jealous God. He will not share His glory. In Exodus 20:3, He tells us that we are not to have any other gods before him. He knows that we can be very skeptical about matters of faith - we want to see before we believe. Physically, we can see ourselves and others, but we cannot see Him. It is a natural tendency to trust what we see and disbelieve that which we do not see. The irony of this misplaced trust is that we have disappointed ourselves time and time again. How can we insist on putting trust in that which we know to be fallible. Once we trust in the Wonderful Counselor, whom we do not see, He will never forsake us. He is infallible. David encourages us in Psalm 27: "When my father and my mother forsake me, then the Lord will take me up." *Asaph*, the Hebrew translation of the word "take," in this instance, carries with it the connotation of removing, fetching, or recovering.

If you find yourself in an abandoned or desperate situation, your best hope is for someone to come by and snatch you up and out, to furnish your immediate rescue. I don't want you to envision some "Hollywoodesque" love affair, where He is extending His hand in slow motion, smiling at you as you squeeze it, shuddering with anticipation. No, this is more like drowning and being encircled by sharks, going under for the final time. It is under these circumstances that He comes by and takes your hand and snatches you out of the hand of the enemy. This is the God of our fathers and of our future:

> He brought me up also out of an horrible pit,
> out of the miry clay, and set my feet upon a rock,
> and established my goings.
>   Psalm 40:2

He offered His Son as a ransom for you. There is no greater love than sacrificing your life for another. This reminds me of a story where a little boy was going to provide blood to his young sister, by means of a transfusion. As he lay on the operating table, biting his lip, he bravely asked the doctor how many more minutes he had to live. It was then that the doctor realized the child thought they were going to drain all of his blood to give it to his sister.

One of the amazing things about God's grace is that he gives it freely and unconditionally. Sometimes parents, in their zeal to believe in the honor of their child, may go overboard in defending their precious one, insisting that a particular accusation cannot be true. "My child would never do something like that!" When the dust settles and the child is home, the parents may privately change their questioning tactics to: "You didn't do that - did you?" Here is arguably one of the most awesome things about God - He knows we are guilty and He spares us anyway.

Guilty of what you ask? Guilty of putting ourselves before Him or of living lifestyles that dislodge, disregard, or dishonor Him. Many of us are guilty of trusting more in ourselves than we do Him. In the midst of our worldly accolades, the light of success can shine so brightly that your reflection is the only one you see. He tells us plainly in Deuteronomy 8:17 - 19:

And thou say in thine heart,
My power and the might of mine hand,
Hath gotten me this wealth.

But thou shalt remember the Lord thy God:
for it is He that giveth thee power to get wealth,
That He may establish His covenant
which He sware unto thy fathers, as it is this day.

And it shall be, if thou do at all forget the Lord thy God, and walk after other gods, and serve them, and worship them, I testify against you this day that ye shall surely perish.

Oh, you thought it was all your overtime and diligence that got you that promotion? Or perhaps you thought it was your connections or skills that helped you to move to the next level. Au contraire, mon ami - this is the truest case of "it's not what you know, it's Who you know."

The reason our denial of Him is so critical is that when we try to supersede Him, we are completely out of focus on every decision that we make. Whoever is sitting on our throne, in this key position of authority in our life, will determine our course of action as well as our final destination. We may have internal struggles in trying to come to terms with letting Him rule, but as we are evolving to that point of revelation, that does not negate His power or authority over our life. It is like not believing that the earth is round. Just because many people did not subscribe to the truth, that did not make it any less legitimate. The interesting thing about truth is that it always rises to the top - it's appearance is just a matter of timing. There shall come a time when all the debates shall go out the window and all the philosophers and wise doubters shall be silenced and then, Paul says it best in Romans 14:11, "As I live, saith the Lord, every knee shall bow to me, and every tongue shall confess to God."

When you are bowing, believing and confessing to God, that is not the time to seek Him as your Counselor. If you wait that long, you are about one life time too late. Let's examine the benefit of the present election of His counsel and propitiation. This word propitiation refers to the idea of Christ serving as the sacrifice for your sin. He stands in your place as client, counselor, and condemned one. Because Christ is the only offering that could stand in your place, when you think about it, that says a lot about your value. Not just any old sacrifice would do - the exchange for your valuable life had to be something both perfect and priceless. And that is when Christ, in all His glory said, "Send Me."

~~~~~~

Christ is the only offering that could stand in for you.

~~~~~~

One sound that tickles my ear and makes me shake my head in amazement is that of a professional auctioneer practicing his craft. The skill and the speed of his voice, are simply remarkable. The auctioneer's job and our intrinsic, God-planted value remind me of an illustrative poem penned by Myra Brooks Welch:

The Touch of the Master's Hand

Twas battered and scarred, and the auctioneer
Thought it scarcely worth his while
To waste much time on the old violin,
But held it up with a smile.
"What am I bidden, good folks," he cried,
"Who will start bidding for me?"
"A dollar, a dollar. Then two! Only two?
Two dollars, and who'll make it three?"
"Three dollars, once; Three dollars, twice;
"Going for three ..." But no,
From the room, far back, a gray-haired man
Came forward and picked up the bow;

Then wiping the dust from the old violin,
And tightening the loose strings.
He played a melody pure and sweet
As sweet as a caroling angel sings.
The music ceased and the auctioneer
With a voice that was quiet and low,
Said, "What am I bidden for the old violin?"
And he held it up with the bow.
"A thousand dollars, and who'll make it two?

Two thousand! And who'll make it three?
Three thousand, once; three thousand twice;
And going, and gone!" said he.
The people cheered, but some of them cried,
"We do not quite understand
What changed its worth?" Swift came the reply:
"The touch of the master's hand."

And many a man with life out of tune,
And battered and scarred with sin,
Is auctioned off cheap to the thoughtless crowd,
Much like the old violin.
A "mess of pottage," a glass of wine;
A game -- and he travels on.
He's "going" once, and "going" twice,
He's "going" and "almost gone."
But the Master comes and the foolish crowd
Never can quite understand
The worth of a soul and the change that is wrought
By the touch of the Master's hand.

In our individual journeys of coming to appreciate our value, we come to realize that we cannot afford an attorney - the price is too high. We can only thank God that He extends to us the grace and mercy to represent us, in spite of us. He has sent His Son to plead your case and even in the pronouncement of your "Guilty" verdict, your Counselor is allowing you to go free. What do you do now?

You can trust Him;
Just Him.
Can He trust you,
With the things that matter?

Released on Your Own Recognizance

Recognizance is an interesting word. When you dissect it into its Latin root, you are bringing together "re" which means again and "cognoscere" which means to know. Together this combination is a depiction of a fresh start. It's like saying, you are getting to know yourself again. The first time was just a dress rehearsal - you were hiding in the shadows of the person you were meant to be. But this new introduction and knowledge of yourself is the first time you will meet your real, accurate, true self.

This emancipation has to be similar to the feeling that overcame the freed slaves of the Southern United States when they were told that by law they were now liberated. The rumors and hopes had been rampant; they had dared to believe in a legal escape, a way out. And when it came, oh, the celebrations they must have had. When the revelry and loud rejoicing quieted down, they must have looked at one another and questioned, now what? Where do we go? Who's going to take care of us? As horrible as their past had been, to some, an unknown future also promised an element of fear.

The future to a new Christian can also appear frightening - you are in a new relationship and you want to make the best impression. The honeymoon phase is typically exciting and vibrant and you want to tell everyone of your wonderful rescue. The doors have been opened, the shackles removed, and now, you are free to go. The independence you so desperately craved is now yours. A free man or woman! Wow! In this case, your Emancipator is the truth! He says it plainly in John 8:32 - and you shall know the truth, and the truth shall make you free. Well, what are you free to do now? Is this the moment where you can now make your own choices and be accountable only to yourself? When you know who you are in Christ, you are free to reach your fullest potential. You are free to enter into levels of understanding and wisdom that earlier, made no sense to you. You are free from sin and now are a servant of God. Paul tells us that we have reached a new level of excellence - Galatians 5:13 challenges us to use our new position:

> For brethren, ye have been called unto liberty;
> only use not liberty for an occasion to the flesh,
> but by love serve one another.

Here is the great paradox - one would think we'd be freed to do what we want to do. But God, by His examples, has already established that no man is to be an island unto himself. His pattern was to create us for Him and to restore us to a condition whereby we would put others before ourselves. I once knew of a young lady named Joy - she said her name was a constant reminder of her correct priorities as a Christian. J-O-Y represented to her, Jesus first, Others, second, and Yourself last. When we do this, He takes care of us on the back end. (Matthew 19:30)

There is a difference between an attitude of service versus one of martyrdom. Some Christians get so caught up in their serving others that one would think that if they stepped out of the equation, the growth of modern day Christianity would come to a screeching halt. The key to the correct balance lies in the first part of our Joy relationship with our Father. The main part of putting Him first, positions us to commune with Him on a regular and consistent basis. When He has your ear, and you, His, He will reveal to you how much you should put on your plate. He will identify your profitable seasons of heightened activity, in different areas of your life. He is a God of decency and order. You are His ambassador - He doesn't want you running to and fro from project to project, accomplishing nothing, yet supposedly doing it all in His name. You represent Him - He is a God of peace, prosperity, productivity, and perspective. Your are His child and you bear His name. Your Christian walk does not have to be a guessing game; He has left a very explicit manual for your study and application. The only secret is to read and heed.

You are God's ambassador.

In addition to His manual, God has also provided an Internal Advisor, to help you stay on your course. This is what Jesus told the disciples, in the 14th chapter of John:

I will not leave you **comfortless** - Greek translation, *orphano*, means bereaved, fatherless. (John 14:18);

The Comforter, which is the Holy Ghost, whom the Father will send in my name, he shall teach you all things, and bring all things to your remembrance, whatsoever I have said unto you. (John 14:26)

This information is so vital because we need to be reminded that we do have a great calling on our life. During times of stress or confusion, we may feel abandoned, lost, or doubtful, but God has already told us that He is not a deadbeat dad but rather a father who is the model for all fathers. He will never leave you and He will bring to the front of your mind sweet reassurances that He planted there earlier. You must spend time with Him so He can do both the planting and uprooting. I'm not much of a gardener, but even I know that you have to remove rocks, weeds, and other growth inhibitors before you throw seeds down to grow new plants. Similarly, God will kill the weeds of self-hatred, self-deception, confusion and mediocrity. He will plant in you a new crop of excellence, integrity, holiness, and humility. He is on your side. He wants your success even more than you. He is your greatest cheerleader. He created you to be a winner.

You are now free, in Christ. Free to do what? Free to live. Free to become a three dimensional person. Free to stop sleep walking through life. When you really get a hold of the fact that you are part of God's plan, you will just marvel on His greatness and if you are smart, you will begin to seek His face and His mission for your life.

In the beginning was the Word, and the Word was with God and the Word was God (John 1:1). Centuries ago, before you were even a sparkle in your daddy's eye, God had you on His mind. As time has unfolded itself over the past several thousand years, God has been preparing a place for you to make your entrance onto center stage. His timing is so magnificent, that He didn't introduce you one decade too soon or one moment too late. The attending physicians may have even had to make the emergency decision to induce labor, to hasten your arrival, but through it all, you were born exactly when God said it was time for you to show up. He is not only an on time God, but everything He does is on time. He has a plan for your life and He is so meticulous in His details, that even the split second when you came screaming into this world, was preordained.

The question begs to be answered - Do you matter that much? And from the depths of my soul, I must respond with a hearty, glorious, resounding YES! God has a plan for your life! You matter to Him and your presence here, at this time, in your family, in your community, has been divinely ordained. Your are holding a specially designed hand of cards - what shall your next move be? How have you played your hand so far? Are you fulfilling your purpose? If you were to get a mid-term review, would your Creator be pleased? Are you at least on target? Are you where He wants you to be? You see, you may have some questions for Him, but it is likely He has some questions for you as well. Questions like - why didn't you step out on faith? I prepared a place for you in the presence of your enemies - why didn't you dine? When I called you, why did you look the other way? When I told you to speak, why didn't you open your mouth and when I told you to be quiet, why didn't you hold your tongue? His questions of course would all be rhetorical since He already knows your thoughts, fears, and motives.

God wants your success even more than you do.

You are on His mind and He wants the best for you - when He reflects on your design and your purpose, He wants you to know that He made you a little lower than the angels, and that He has crowned you with glory and honor. Psalm 139 reminds us of the tenderness of the Father's thoughts towards you, His child:

How precious also are thy thoughts unto me, O God!
how great is the sum of them!
If I should count them,
they are more in number than the sand...
                                                    verses 17-18

I will praise thee: for I am fearfully and
wonderfully made: marvelous are thy works...
                                                    verse 14

The exciting aspect about walking this life journey, is that we cannot see around the next corner. God specializes in leading us through and strengthening us along the way. How must we then respond? My suggestion is simple - we ought to come out with our hands up - raised high in the air - trusting Him wholeheartedly.

The symbolism of raised hands is two fold. Firstly, they represent surrender - opening oneself to the other party in a trusting manner. Raised hands are akin to waving a white flag and saying to the opposing side - I am yours - you have my permission to do with me what you wish. A second significance of raised hands is outright praise. That "You are worthy praise" that comes out when no words can fill the space. Those raised hands are responsive - you may wave them back and forth as you reflect on your life and recall the victories He has won for you. Or they may be ejaculatory in nature - that - "couldn't keep my hands down if I tried to," praise. This praise may be in response to an event in your immediate past that causes you to honor Him in this Spirit-filled, overflowing fashion.

I am challenging you to take your praise to the next level. This level of praise is actually a combination of the two styles just mentioned. This praise stance is what you do after praying - you have communed with Him in your private, innermost thoughts - now you are ready to face the world and its vacillating standards.

When I was a child, I played a jump rope game, whereby two players would hold the ends of the rope and the third player's goal was to jump across, without making contact with the rope. Now, in a stationary position, that objective is rather unintimidating, but the two rope holders main function was to vigorously shake the rope, making it appear like a slippery, slithering snake. Well, I declare that is how the standards of the world are today - they seem to be certain and predict-able on one day and then when you turn around, they have been repositioned and redefined. And like the little girl trying to safely cross, we find that we fall, trip and bruise ourselves, as we miscalculate the rhythm and speed of the vibrations. This is why it is absolutely key to use God's standard as your standard. His word says that He is unchanging - He is the same yesterday, today and forever.

If you want to be successful you must realize that a reliable standard is key and a righteous standard is critical. In a world of changing values and fleeting ideals, God is the only standard that can withstand the fluctuations of the world. When you join God's volunteer army, your future is sure and your final destination is certain. It is like skipping to the final chapter of an exciting book and then going back to the second chapter to see exactly how the story unfolds. We know it is a terrific ending, yet we still cringe as we see our self, as the main character, confronted with taxing situations.

This course that we are put on as we fulfill our various roles, is sometimes overbearing, nerve-wracking, and challenging, but above all, it is ours. I cannot run in your lane, nor you in mine. What God has for you is yours - I cannot take it and probably could not handle it. One of the ways His greatness shows through is in the way He personalizes our course, our blessings, and our tolerance levels. It is interesting to me that the same thing can happen to ten different people and as many as ten different responses could result. We are fearfully and wonderfully made - not just as a human race, but also, as individuals - we owe so much to the One who uniquely crafted us, one by one.

We recently had an ant challenge in my house - I bought a pesticide to exterminate the critters and as I read the directions on the label, I had to shake my head in amazement. It said, "This product is effective against: Pharaoh ants, Cornfield Ants, Fire Ants, Argentine Ants, and a variety of household ants." God is so amazing and so infinite in His creation style. He did not create just one ant and then move on to the next insect - He exercised abundance and diversity even in the design of the seemingly unimportant ant. Now if He is that creative in the animal kingdom how much more do you think He has in His sights for us? He did not stop at just man and woman and set up a cookie cutter prototype. His plan was much more excellent. As similar as we appear in the physical sense, we are strikingly unique in our design. However, our common purpose, is singular - we have been created to honor and glorify our Creator.

Imagine having a neighbor whose child is prospering - socially, emotionally and financially. Your child on the other hand, is still trying to find himself and has made several poor choices along the way. What glory do you receive when you hear of the accolades of the neighbor's child? You may be happy and excited for the parents and pleased in a general sense, but those pleasant thoughts do not excite your heart in the same way as if it were your own child. There is no ownership, no bloodline, when the fruit is not from your household. The same is true for God's family. Many people say, "We are all God's children." That statement has limited truthfulness. We have all been created by God, that is an event we could not control. What is in our hands is the choice to become part of His eternal family. Once in His family, we receive instructions on our rights and responsibilities as family members.

In order to get the right answers that will guide you to a successful life and a glorious eternity, you must be connected to your manufacturer. Do you consult the directions to your washing machine when you want to know how to set up your DVD player? Of course not - you go to the manufacturer, because you are expecting clear instructions as well as some troubleshooting guidance. Our relationship with God should be no different.

We have the privilege of taking an active role in the development of a personal, one on one relationship with our Creator. This relationship is characterized by two way communication, obedience, sacrifice, discipline and growth. This is where a lot of people miss the mark. They get caught up in rituals, rules and responsibilities, all the while neglecting relationship. I talked to a young lady in church and asked her if she knew God. Her automatic answer was a quick yes. Out of curiosity I then asked how long she had been saved. The next phrase sent up the flares, as it does every time I hear it - "for a long time - since I was a baby." The truth of the matter is in most cases, the time of joining God's family is a demarcation in one's life. It is a before and after moment. This is not to say you will necessarily hear trumpet blasts and angels shouting from on high, but to know God is to love Him. And if you know Him you will recognize His love and mercy and you will know when you came in out of the rain.

In the physical sense, a person can feel relief when they are finally dry, sitting in front of the fire place and sipping hot cocoa. Likewise, the renewed, regenerated Christian also recognizes this new sanctuary where a rejuvenated soul has taken up residence. The engine that will drive you to success is the Spirit of God residing in you. There is nothing magical or mysterious about this transformation - it is merely a response on your part, to a God who is yearning for you to be receptive to His calling.

God has a proven track record - He makes no apologies because He makes no mistakes. God is faithful. His Holy Spirit is constantly seeking an avenue to drive down in order to demonstrate His glory. He is in you - you must release Him. What is the most important action that you can take as an empowered believer? The one single action that will guarantee your success is to move - move out of His way. Do not try to box God into your comfort zone - He will not fit. He says in Jeremiah 32:27, "I am the Lord, the God of all mankind. Is anything too hard for me?"

As you move out of His way, remember that your goal should not be the most obvious one - to move closer to your desired result. The winning, one size fits all goal is to seek His face; focus on moving closer to Him. You want peace? Move closer to God. Want prosperity? Move closer to God. Want joy? Move closer to God. Want wisdom? Move closer to God. These attributes are the fruit of His Spirit. The things you want, He not only has, but He is - that is why He is also known as "Yahweh." This name for God means that He is exactly who you need Him to be for you, at any given time. As you make it your constant goal to develop and appreciate an intimate relationship with your Lord and Savior, you will find yourself surrounded by Truth, Abundance, and Creativity. You will become fruitful, passionate, and bold as you find yourself drinking from the saucer because your cup will surely be running over.

He wants His glory to shine so He will do His part to bring it to the forefront of the stage. You must choose to shine your light on Him. His abundant outpouring is perpetual and unstoppable. Well, actually there is one thing that will surely slow Him down and it actually has less to do with Him than it does you. Your attitude of doubt can slow down, dissipate, or even negate the onset of His blessing. He says that it is not if He can, it (the manifested blessing) depends on whether you believe. The employment of certain personality traits and behaviors can actually grease the skids that invite Him to move on your behalf:

a. bull dog faith - the kind that won't let go regardless of what the world is saying and doing;
b. integrity; and
c. trust and obedience

As you concentrate on the development of these attributes, you will find yourself close enough to hear His voice when He speaks. Then you can respond with confidence and wisdom when He directs your path. Any house or home, character or life built without God at the center is worthless anyway so you may as well make Him the head of the construction site of whatever you are trying to erect. His plans are flawless; His tools are versatile and His budget is unlimited. He can do more with one grain of sand than you can do with an entire beach - He is absolutely amazing.

He saved us, by paying a debt we could never pay. If He did nothing else for us, His ultimate sacrifice far outweighs any gift we could ever receive or expect. One might think that is the end of His gift giving, but I guess that is why He refers to Himself as the Alpha and the Omega - the beginning and the end. He not only blesses you by standing at the door and knocking, but upon entering, He changes everything - He restores things, to their original condition. We know the value of that act. People pay thousands of dollars to restore furniture and houses to their original states. How much more valuable are you to your Father in heaven?

God is faithful and His steps are sure. He commands respect and honor and glory because of who He is. Once you surrender and pledge to Him your allegiance - what do you do next? Our entire existence comes down to one word - relationship. How you feel about and (dis)honor God will determine much of where you will end up - in both the natural and spiritual senses.

God wants us to be in fellowship with Him. His definition of a relationship with Him is a two way street. He is a God who actually allows us to express our deepest thoughts to Him and understands us even in the midst of our own confusion and indecisiveness. What about if during the confusion all you hear from Him is silence? I recently received some physical advice that actually meets this spiritual need. A health expert said that when you are craving a late night snack and you can feel your body yearning, almost reaching for satisfaction, that is the time to ignore it the most. In the absence of feeding the urge, your body is forced to turn to its fat storages and satisfy itself in a healthier manner. It is the same with your spiritual "hunger pangs". When you feel that God is not answering you quickly enough, oftentimes that is His Spirit creating a space of time where He can commune with your spirit.

If He cannot draw on the reserves because of their absence, then He will go in and build you up, from the inside out. Romans 8:16 tells us that the Spirit bears witness with our spirit. And instead of running to the mall, or to friends, family or food, we have that wonderful opportunity to just be still and know that He is God. He may even use someone in your path to bless you and yet - that person is not your source. Another name we use when referring to God, is Jehovah-jireh, which literally means, God the Provider. Because God so highly regards relationships, He repeatedly puts us in situations where we are driven, forced, or led to help one another.

This reminds me of a story shared with me about a faithful tenant and her non-believing landlord. It seems as though this woman had fallen on hard times and could barely pay the rent or even purchase food for her family. Seeing the apparent absence of this God who was supposed to be the provider of this woman's needs, the insensitive landlord relished the opportunity to dangle this financially embarrassing situation over her. To make matters worse, he decided to go to the market and purchase enough food for a month, so he could appear as her savior and really make her God look bad. So, once he bought it, he snuck into her apartment and filled her kitchen with all the food. When she returned home, and saw the miracle, she immediately began praising God and exclaiming His goodness! The landlord ran down stairs to confront the woman. When she told him what had happened, how the food miraculously appeared, and how good her God was, he cut her off and interrupted, "Hmpf - you say your God is so good and comes through for you, but I can tell you for sure that He is not reliable, doesn't perform miracles and I still say, probably does not even exist - He did not save you - I did! I bought all this food for you to show you that your God is a farce - now what do you think about that?!" After a moment of silence, the woman of faith responded, "Well, He used a fool to bless me, so I say that He has proven Himself yet again!"

While you are waiting on your miracle, what should you be doing - how should you occupy your time? This period of silence can indeed evoke anxiety, frustration, or discouragement. Your faith becomes your anchor - it holds you steady through the storm. Turn the situation around in your favor - know that this is a building period. God has a frequent modus operandi, whereby He works from the inside out. To the casual observer it may look like no change is taking place. But I like to borrow a page from one of God's oldest examples - conception.

During this miraculous event, not even the two involved parties know the exact moment when their respective contributions cross paths. And so the change begins. From the outside looking on, it is imperceptible to the human eye.

However, after the passage of a couple of weeks, the transformation cannot be denied. The mother's lack of the initial knowledge of her new condition, does not negate the alteration. The seeds of growth are on their way. And similarly, just because you cannot witness God's hand changing your situation, that does not mean He is not actively unfolding solutions to your current challenges.

Truly, it is during some of these quiet moments where the silence seems to be mocking us. The absence of an answer is practically deafening. Oftentimes these can actually become Defining Moments. Events where if we hold on just a little while longer, we see we some of His most magnificent manifestations. Can you imagine how it must have been before the beginning of time? Ominous, dark vastness, filled with vapors and silence and if you had been around to speak, your voice would only echo endlessly. And then, at His set time, God said, "Let there be light." The very first sunrise must have been something to behold! Just as it was dark before the dawn, so you must, during your dark hours, entreat God to empower you to hold on, until His set time.

Sometimes there may be something within your power that affects the ushering in of His solution. In other words, He may be waiting on your obedience in a smaller or even unrelated area. Other times, you may just be a drafted volunteer from the audience, who will be used to help another person move on to their next level. Believe it or not, it is not always about you. Just like God uses others to bless you, yes you too are used by Him, to bless others.

As you are watching a particular situation unfold, which route should you take to minimize obstacles and ensure victory? In 2 Chronicles 20:15, the Lord says:

> Be not afraid nor dismayed by reason of
> this great multitude; for the battle is not yours,
> but God's."

I am an avid fan of police thrillers and I cannot help but picture myself in some of the scenarios. During the investigative stages when they are trying to rebuild the crime scene they always ask the victim, "Who would have done this - do you have any enemies?" I always thought this line of questioning would be ineffective if I were in the scenario. I figured I am a nice person with many friends and no sworn enemies. As I continue to study the Word of God, I am now convinced that I have a multitude of enemies on my track, the chief of whom, is the devil himself. Anything he can do to defeat, deter, or detain me, is a ploy that he will use.

There is indeed a great multitude against me and against you - the collective goal is to thwart God's plan, now that you are on His side. Understanding this one thing can make the difference between your winning and losing the battle. Know that while you are waiting on your answer from God, the true battle is between two opponents - and you are not even one of them. The battle is the age old struggle between Faith and Fear. These adversaries are mutually exclusive and they look to you for routine feedings. The fear component that is so integral to our success and growth is knowing that any fear that is meant to harm us, is not of God. Reflecting on our being fearfully made, it is extraordinary that He built in us, a fight or flight instinct designed for the benefit of our survival. But fear of stepping out of your comfort zone, or of a doctor's report, or an upcoming test - these types of fears are not authored by God. He tells us in 2 Timothy 1:7 that He has not given us the spirit of fear, but of love, and power, and of a sound mind.

We see great examples of powerful, obedient men and women of God listed in the eleventh chapter of Hebrews. Their actions were documented in part so that we could see by example, what active faith looks like. This chapter on faith starts out with a simple definition: faith is the substance of things hoped for, the evidence of things not seen. The corollary to that point is that if you can see something with your eyes, then it's not faith - in that case, the physical proof of the thing seen, is what gives us the assurance. The God faith on the other hand, deals with the Who instead of the what. God's record is so solid, so that all we have to do is rewind our mental recorders, to remind ourselves of His faithfulness. And while we're at it, we may as well do some freeze frames - remembering how many times God showed up in the past when the victory was nowhere in sight. He specializes in turning situations around and redefining circumstances, creating solutions that prior to His arrival, weren't even part of your vocabulary.

In modern day vernacular we would say He is a God of sequels - when you think the show is over, He steps out in all His glory and directs the next scene. He can take a little of nothing and make something out of it. Just ask the little boy who donated his three small fish and five loaves of bread to feed over 5,000 people. One of the best aspects I enjoy about that story is that God provided more than enough for that crowd - at the end of the meal, the disciples ran around with baskets collecting leftovers, and the extra victuals added up to even more than the original three fish and five loaves. I know now, more than ever before, why the seasoned, senior saints call Him the Way maker.

I have heard innumerable Christians sharing testimonies of healings, surprise financial blessings, vanishing illnesses, and wholeness replacing brokenness. We have our plans but God has The Plan. The Plan is always the best plan for us because He has access to other variables we are unable to consider. For example, God can weigh our very hearts which deal with our motives, our tendencies, and our greatest expectations. He can also factor in the past, present, and future, as it relates to our well-being. He knows what is around every corner and He enables us to meet and deal with the unexpected. One of the biggest variables He measures is our faith. Let's take a look at His estimation of the value of faith. Habakkuk 2:4 tells us:

> Behold, his soul which is lifted up
> is not upright in him:
> But the just shall live by his faith.

Understanding that we are created in God's image and that He is a triune God, we can see the parallel in how He created us in a tri-part manner:

Him	**us**
Father	soul
Son	body
Holy Spirit	spirit

We know that progress cannot be made in a schizophrenic fashion - if the whole moves forward, the parts must be in agreement. How can your body move forward when one foot wants to go right and the other left? The result would be utter chaos and you would end up flat on your face. Likewise it is with the soul, body, and spirit.

One direction -- One accord -- One purpose -- One victory

God just told us, through Habakkuk that the man whose soul is lifted up, i.e. prideful, has in him a soul that is not upright. Now picture that - you are trying to move forward and your soul is in a prone position. How easy is it to drag a body across the finish line? Contrarily, picture the three parts in alignment and on one accord, seeking and following God's plan. In this second picture I see the momentum of obedience uplifting the Christian and helping him to finish the race in a strong manner, because all parts are moving in sync.

The second part of that passage addresses the fruit of the Christian's faith. We do not want to minimize the power of these two little words - "shall live." The Hebrew translation for live is chayah, which means, to stay alive, to be preserved, to flourish, to enjoy life; to live in happiness, to breathe, to be animated, to recover health. The Spirit-Filled Bible says the fundamental idea is to "live and breathe," breathing being the evidence of life in the Hebrew concept. This is a rather convincing impression - think about it - if you are not breathing, you are not living! Period.

Chayah magnifies the idea in our minds so we can realize a higher quality of life. We have to only look at the converse to realize the positive power we have in the palm of our hands.

The Old Testament was written describing events before the appearance of Jesus Christ. Many passages were penned in command format - that was the way the boundaries for behavior were outlined. Along that vein, Habakkuk could have easily read: and those who do not have faith shall live a life characterized by death, decrease, depression and disease. I enjoy Habakkuk's wording because it allows us to focus on the blessings rather than the curses. Now seeing both sides of the same coin, the next logical question is - what person in their right mind, would choose to live, relying mostly on his own wisdom and without faith? That person has nothing to gain and everything to lose.

The obedient Christian will finish the race strong.

In the book of Matthew, we find Jesus chastising the listeners regarding their doubting God's ability or concern to take care of them. In chapter 6, verse 30, He says:

> If God so clothe the grass of the field,
> which today is, and tomorrow is cast
> into the oven, shall He not much more
> clothe you, O ye of little faith?

The Greek word for **faith** in this instance is *oligopistos*, which describes a faith that is underdeveloped. In any other circumstance where under development is the condition, we try to come to the rescue of the victim. When it comes to third world countries, we make efforts to send food or teachers or technology in order to help make improvements. If the situation is more individual in nature and we are dealing with people who are not meeting their potential, we make available the necessary training to help them in their development. In the same manner, Jesus is saying that it is unacceptable for us to wield little faith. He does not want you to walk around with weak muscles. Why choose to be a spiritual wimp of little faith when you have the potential to possess great faith?

We see the exercising of this level of faith when Jesus visited the town of Capernaum and was approached by a centurion desperately needing assistance. He cried unto Jesus, saying his servant was paralyzed and tormented and needed healing from The Master. Jesus agreed to go to him and heal him. The centurion said, "Oh no - that's too much to ask of you - just speak the word and I know he will be healed." Upon seeing his faithfulness, in Matthew 8:13 Jesus remarked, "as you have believed, so let it be done for you."

This example in Matthew is a fundamental key to walking in relationship with Christ. This same word for **believe**, translated as *pisteuo* is also found in Romans 10:9. This familiar passage reads, "If you confess with your mouth and believe in your heart, you shall be saved." This most basic, simple embracing of believing, means to be fully convinced, to acknowledge, to rely on. Pisteuo is more than credence in church doctrines or articles of the faith. It expresses reliance upon and a personal trust that produces obedience. It includes submission and a positive confession of the lordship of Jesus Christ. This was the faith exchanged by the centurion for the healing of his servant. Notice the fact that the one who needed the healing was not the one who actually exercised the faith in the presence of Jesus. It excites me to realize that our great faith can actually be the bridge to someone else's healing. Step back and examine your relationships. Do you see any displays of underdeveloped faith that may actually be standing between someone else and their breakthrough?

My brother is a personal trainer and he tells me the longer you stay away from the gym, the more challenging it is to get back in shape. It is no different when it comes to our spiritual side. The more time we spend away from God, not reading His Word, not spending time praising Him in harmony and fellowship with other Christians, and most importantly, not seeking His counsel through prayer, the harder it is to take that leap to get back into spiritual fitness. What gymnasium can we attend to build up our faith muscle? I know of personal trainers who come to your home for private fitness lessons. They will work within your schedule to help you meet your mark. God has a better plan - He will meet you in the seclusion of your home, for one on one instruction - and He does not charge by the hour. Romans 10:17 says, faith comes by hearing and hearing by the word of God. How can you increase your faith? Listen to more of God's Word - this quantity issue will raise the quality of your life. Finally when you spend quiet time with Him, He will also whisper things into your spirit - secrets to your success. He wants to give you daily counsel, not just rescue instructions. God is a proactive God whose wisdom can keep you out of a lot of trouble on the front end. It is our partial trust in Him that gets us in trouble.

The choice we make to begin to walk by faith, has the potential of developing into a beautiful, intimate love affair with our Creator. As we faithfully reach out to him we are given greater revelation of His faithfulness towards us. Deuteronomy 7:9 says, "know that the Lord your God, He is God, the faithful God, who keeps covenant and mercy for a thousand generations with those who love Him and keep His commandments." Any way you look at it, a thousand generations is a long time. When was the last time you kept your word for a season, much less for a generation? You know what I mean - the flippant "let's do lunch" promises, the casual, "I'll call you next week" comments, or the fleeting "I'll pray for you" statements. Most of these utterances reflect good intentions, but our weak, mortal selves come up short in the area of follow through. This is one aspect that is so wondrous about God - if He says it, He means it. You can count on His integrity.

The apostle Paul tells us that not only is the Lord faithful, but He will also establish us and guard us from the evil one. Paul reminds us of the dance - the call and response relationship we have with Christ. As with any great dance duo, there has to be a leader and and a follower. The skill of the leader makes the couple look graceful. Let us purpose to not get the roles confused. Examine the following illustration drawn out in 2 Timothy 2: 11-13:

This is a faithful saying	(believe this)
(cost) For if we died with Him	(our old sinful nature)
(benefit)We shall also live with Him	(now/eternally)
(cost) If we endure	(hang in there)
(benefit)We shall also reign with Him	(in eternity)
(cost) If we deny Him	(pride)
(penalty)He also will deny us	(before God)
(cost) If we are faithless,	(opt to live without Him)
(benefit) He remains faithful;	(His promises stand)

(standard) He cannot deny Himself.

It is priceless to be able to turn to an excellent standard that does not change. It is reassuring to be able to serve a God of integrity who says what He means and means what He says.

Just as His Word says that faith without works is dead, He gives us vivid examples that we may see the result of active faith. First John 1:9 says that if we confess our sins, He is faithful and just to forgive our sins and cleanse us from all unrighteousness. His faithfulness is a catalyst that causes His pure, merciful heart to be responsive to our sinful hearts. He hears our confession and His faithfulness, coupled with His grace, moves Him to forgive us, cleanse us, renew us, and bring us back into fellowship with Him. He is so faithful to His Word that there is no time where someone could do something so heinous, that He would say, "Oh no, I will not forgive that - you have gone too far." What reveals God's faith the most? Our humility. He is abundantly restorative in His nature, when we admit that we:

a) cannot do it without Him;
b) regret having left Him; or
c) misrepresented Him and are seeking another chance

He loves to be in relationship with us - that is why He made us! We come to Him in faith - He receives us and restores us by faith, i.e. because He said He would. Every time He picks us up and brushes us off, He is returning us to the starting line, repositioning us to run the race, reach our potential, and fulfill our purpose. No other manufacturer can or would do that - they'd sooner throw in the towel and go back to the drawing board. You would give up on Him before He would turn His back on you. Impossible, you say? He's done too much for you? Let's ask Peter what it feels like to watch the Messiah perform miracles for three years and then, when accused of consorting with Him, he denied the relationship. Never say never. This is a living example of why you need to stay basked in the Word and in fellowship with God. When Satan or his minions do attack you, your mind will already have a prepared statement - there will be no "catching you off guard."

I beckon you to raise yourself to an offensive posture and come out of your prayer closet, with your hands up! Raise them in victory. Come out of your front door with your hands up! Get out of your car, with your hands up! Come out of your cubicle at work, with your hands up! It is time to surrender to Him all that you do not want to deal with - which by the way, should be everything. God wants to take care of you, moment by moment, and day by day.

Instead of throwing your hands up in a gesture of anger and frustration, throw them up in a covenant of surrender and praise. "Lord, this is yours - I can't deal with it!" "God, this situation has your name written all over it - let me move out of the way!" "Father, I thank you for the victory you are performing even now as I am surrendering this situation to you!" Instead of coming out of your corner fighting, come out with your hands up, so He can show His handiwork.

One thing we can be very good at is our ability to be stubborn and hard headed. One of the proverbs of my childhood days was, "A hard head makes a soft behind." God may have a different way of dealing with us that is not as apparent as physical discipline, but He does have a way of getting our attention. We may experience moments of deja vu as we repeat the same mistakes over and over. He does not make a habit of forcing Himself on us - that is why He gave us a free will. He wants us, through applied wisdom, to make the best choices for our lives. The first smart choice we can make is to align ourselves with Him. I heard a speaker say once, in remarking about the uncertainties of life, "There are no guarantees in this life - as a matter of fact, I am sure of only two things: 1) There is a God and 2) I am not Him." In stepping back to realize our place in this seemingly infinite cosmos, it is good to know that there is a specific blueprint for each of our lives. God has a plan for you and the first part of the plan involves your realization that God has a plan for you. Psalm 100:3 puts it this way:

> Know ye that the Lord he is God:
> it is he that hath made us, and not we ourselves;
> we are his people, and the sheep of his pasture.

To first imagine what key role you play in God's Masterpiece, you must at least have a general appreciation of His previous work. Let's take a brief look at His divine resume, in the area of production and the inner workings of some of His creations. Because you are a Christian, His abundance is already encapsulated in you - you have control of the release valve. God does not have abundance - He is abundance - just like He is love. Abundance is part of His essence. Take a look at the vastness of the universe to put things into perspective.

Our earth is part of the Milky Way galaxy, which consists of at least 200 billion stars. Our sun is just one of those stars and is 92 million miles away from the earth. The surface of the sun is almost 12,000 times greater than the earth's, and the sun's volume is about 1,300,000 times the volume of the earth. That means that if you had a pile of earths and dropped one into the sun every second, filling the sun would take 15 days. The largest star known to man is called Pistol Star. It is 100 times as massive as our sun and 10 million times as bright. This star releases as much energy in 6 seconds, as our sun releases in an entire year. I'm just saying, even in these brief examples, that you must agree that we serve an extravagant God. Do you want more proof? Observe the plentiful species of animals and plants. There are over 20,000 kinds of butterflies and more than 280,000 species of flowering plants. Our God operates in a lavish mode -   He is a God of surplus and creativity - and He lives in you.

The question is not whether or not God is rich - the deeper question is: Can you handle the blessings He sends your way? Everyone seems to want what God has, but if our present accounts are brought current, we might consider turning in some things He has already put in our basket. How is your health - are you taking care of yourself? What about your family - are you making time for your spouse and/or children? How about that house He's given you - not the dream house, but the starter one you have now. Are you cleaning and maintaining that one, with an attitude of thankfulness? Oh, He's definitely in charge of cattle on 10,000 hills, but, He doesn't want you to fritter away something that is supposed to be an asset, after all, His reputation is on the line. When people find out that you are a Christian, they tend to put on their spectacles, to see if you will make a spectacle out of yourself. If they can add another saint to their wall of shame, then of course, that is more ammunition for Satan as he doesn't mind using you as a stumbling block to keep someone away from Christ.

Your job is to reflect a mirror on Him and shine it to the outside world, that they may see Him in you. The challenge, or duplicity comes when people think you are reflecting Him, but they are really just seeing your flesh, walk in its own selfishness. Not having time to run a DNA check, all they have to go on is what they witness in that brief window of time. Similarly, when they see the abundant fruit overflowing in several areas of your life, they may jump to the conclusion that you are meeting great success because of your own knowledge and wisdom. It is your duty to quickly introduce them to your Source. Quickly is the mode, because you don't even want to have the appearance of hesitating when it comes to the Giver of good and perfect gift in your life.

Like He is extravagant in His treatment toward us, so should we be in our treatment to others. Sometimes they don't earn kindness and love - neither do we. Surely they don't always deserve it - neither do we - But God - in spite of ourselves, richly digs deep, and gives us countless measures of grace, mercy, and forgiveness. Psalm 130:3-4 says :

> If you, God, kept records on wrongdoings,
> who would stand a chance?
> As it turns out, forgiveness is your habit,
> And that's why you're worshipped.

We all have habits - what characterizes the fabric of our life is our choice. God chooses to forgive. Again He is leading by example. When others see your overwhelming spirit of kindness, mercy and grace, they will know that there is something different about you. Some say, when they are faced with an unpredictable event, they respond by doing what comes naturally. The more mature response, that is sure to lead to victory, is to do what comes spiritually. One of the current slogans played out in our community today is the term "to represent". In the truest sense of the word, it just means that you are packaging yourself in a way that would create a positive image of the person or organization you are speaking for, perhaps in their absence. Try on some of Webster's definitions for represent:

to be the equivalent of;
    to be a substitute for;
        to serve as a specimen;

to speak and act for by duly conferred authority.

This final definition is one of my personal favorites. This reminds me of the ambassadorship we are called to accept as part of our new role as a member of the body of Christ. We are not to step into this role lightly or receive it as an empty, figurehead position. Instead, He calls us to reign with power, assurance, and authority. To the casual observer, there may be no physical change. Our basic personality is not likely to change - that part which is not contrary to Christ. In explaining this newness to me, one of my teachers once pointed out - if you told corny jokes before you got saved, it's likely you'll still be corny after salvation. That helped me to understand that just as God has so many varieties of butterflies, He also has many personalities in His Christian family.

One of the enjoyable pastimes I have is noticing the positive and obvious change in others. Whether it deals with weight loss, body building, face lifts, or some other stunning improvement, I am excited for the person of all the benefits that lay before them. Below is a possible diagram of the same person, unsaved, then saved:

BEFORE	**AFTER**
fearful	faithful
self-centered	God-centered
dictator-leader	servant-leader
"just getting by" productivity	excellence as standard
leaning on self/others	leaning on God

world dictates standard	God is the standard
no hope/no cup	cup running over
running from God	running to God
building on sand	building on rock

Christ makes all the difference - we have but one obligation once we are saved. We must obey His commandments. First John says if you love me, keep my commandments. This is so essential that if you follow His commandments, everything else will fall in line. The application of faith-filled obedience gives you the pass key to so much more of his wisdom, which in turn will guide you in making profitable decisions in all areas of your life. We are best reminded of this side of God, by Matthew 7:7-11:

Ask, and it shall be given you; seek,
and ye shall find; knock, and it shall
be opened unto you.

For every one that asketh, receiveth;
and he that seeketh findeth; and to
him that knocketh it shall be opened.

Or what man is there of you, whom if
his son ask bread, will he give him a stone?
Or if he ask fish, will he give him a serpent?

If ye then, being evil, know how to give
good gifts unto your children, how much
more shall your Father, which is in heaven
give good things to them that ask him?

My military past brings to my recollection, an analogy that underscores God's magnitude and abundance toward us. His gifts are like a Meal Ready to Eat (MRE). In the absence of finer culinary selections, these pre-packaged food items are provided to soldiers when they go out to conduct training operations. The MRE is completely dehydrated to a compact form, nevertheless, all the ingredients are still present. All the soldier has to do is add water and mix. Looking into the essence of His "wholeness," we are reminded that we are to be a reflection of Him. He is complete in Himself. He is everything He needs to be at any given time, because He is the author of time, so consequent-ly, nothing can ever "come up" without His approval, authority and acquiescence. He is self-sustaining - a God who depends on nothing or nobody. One of the more humbling portions of scripture is Psalm 50:12, where God says, "If I were hungry, I would not tell you - why should He? What can we do for God to satisfy His hunger? How could we quench His thirst? These rhetorical questions bring into focus the reminder that God's completeness is actually shrunken down and replicated in our very souls. All that we need is already inside of us - instead of wasting a lifetime of energy searching for fulfillment outside of our beings, we ought to be on an internal expedition, digging away at the inside, marveling at the wonderment that God has placed in our bosom. We are already   complete, whole, and bursting at the seams, waiting to be discovered.

The confusion is oftentimes heavily masked by a cloak of fear - I believe many people are actually afraid of who they will find once the music stops and the crowd goes away. Who are we really? Do we dare face the silence? The most telling characteristic I have noticed about fear is that it is typically not all it is cracked up to be. The fear demon reminds me greatly of the Wizard of Oz - just a little man behind a grand facade. When you confront fear, you are positioning yourself to move beyond it, to the upper chambers of your soul and the onward journey to your greatness.

The key to tapping into your great spirit is putting the

faith key into the keyhole. We often look at the objective without evaluating the role of the journey. The journey is purposeful and valuable. The challenge with our choices is that we put all the focus either on the objective or the journey - they each have to be measured and appreciated for what they bring to your growth. When your goals are in line with God's plan for your life, and He highlights one and puts it in your sights, there is still a responsibility that rests with you. It is necessary for you to add just two ingredients to get the desired results: Faith and Action. My five year old daughter has recently been reciting an African proverb - "When you pray, move your feet." She is learning early that faith without action is not faith. Faith without action is flat, 2 dimensional, and bland. Faith in motion is exciting, hopeful, expectant, and 4 dimensional. Applied faith causes you to praise God in advance because you are anticipating the full manifestation of His glory. It is akin to sitting in the audience of a premier show waiting for the curtain to rise. Rave reviews have preceded the event and you are sitting on the edge of your front row seat. In your case the rave reviews are the testimony of where He has brought you from. The psalmist says, in Chapter 77:11-12:

> I will remember the deeds of the Lord;
> yes, I will remember your miracles of
> long ago. I will meditate on all your
> works and consider all your mighty deeds.

He has already offered His Son for your sins and given you the gift of eternal life. Everything else is small potatoes. He has given you the best at the beginning of the race. I am told that when a person is racked with pain in a hospital, they sometimes have a device that allows them to release medication into their bloodstream to abate the discom-fort. God is like that - He has placed His Holy Spirit in us to serve as the Comforter, to help us deal with the various situations that come our way. Sometimes, we don't even know how much to ask for - we don't know what to pray - but God, knowing us, because He made us, has even set it up to help us even when we don't know how to pray. His answers and covering are accessible for the duration of the race. He stands ready to richly bless you in the here and now. He wants to shower you, as a testimony to His greatness. You come to Him with a thimble and He wants you to come with a tractor trailer. You insult Him with your minimal requests and minimal obedience.

He has given you the best at the beginning of the race.

Why we are willing to settle for bottom feeding is a mystery. We have the power and free will to control our thought life, which in turn will control our very decisions. I love Paul's bold spirit in 2 Corinthians 10:5:

> Casting down imaginations,
> and every high thing that
> exalteth itself against the knowledge of God,
> and bringing into captivity
> every thought to the obedience of Christ.

This is offensive warfare. You are the gatekeeper of your thoughts. You decide where to focus your attention. Lift your mind up to a level of realization of His key role in your life. Recognize that as your soul provider, He is your Sole Provider and Source of all that is good for you.

He provides blessings for you that you are not even aware of - things that you can easily take for granted. For example, as you read this book, the blood running through your veins and the oxygen traveling its course through your body are both functioning due to the grace of God. The human heart beats

100,800 times each day - how many times today have you stopped to thank Him for the ongoing functioning of that essential organ? It is common to overlook this type of "automatic blessing." Take time out to recognize and appreciate His hand in your life. Where would you be if He left you alone for even five minutes. When you acknowledge His presence you are taking a back seat to being controlled by Self.

The Word tells us not to grieve or quench the Holy Spirit - in other words, stand back, and let Him do His thing. Remember you can do all things through Christ (Philippians 4:13) and likewise, He can do all things through you. If you allow Him to have His way in every area of your life, He will overwhelm you with such blessings that the only lack will be enough room to store them all. To receive His blessings you must stay focused on your role and responsibilities in your relationship with Him. Who is in charge - you or Him? This reminds me of a popular bumper sticker - "God is my co-pilot." That precise attitude is the root of the problem. He does not desire that we share the driving responsibility nor that we slow the journey down by trying to navigate according to our map. He wants us to wholeheartedly hand the controls over to Him, of our own free will. That is the beginning of trust and obedience.

Once you allow Him full control you will realize that He is also the source of versatility. He can address any problem and apply not just any salve, but a Gileadic balm that is uniquely designed for you. That means that you and three friends may be in the midst of similar trials yet He will apply a different antidote to each situation. He is the One who answers to the name of Yahweh - in laymen's terms that means "I am what you need me to be at any given time." Because He is an omniscient God, He has the solution to the current challenge you are facing as well as the key to any problems you may face next week, next month, and next year. He is a God of solutions. Everything you need is in Him and He is in you, therefore you have everything you need to prosper, already inside of you. Psalm 118:24-25 is a familiar passage - at least part of it is. Let us examine it in its entirety:

This is the day which the Lord hath made;
We will rejoice and be glad in it.
Save now, I beseech thee, O Lord:
O Lord, I beseech thee, send now prosperity.

Today is a new day - the slate is clean - He offers this day to you on a silver platter. What will you do with it? It is a gift that first demands appreciation. Many who saw yesterday did not have the privilege to see today's sunrise. So as we rejoice and than God for this day, let us do it mostly through our actions toward others. Be a blessing on this day so that the Lord will see that you truly appreciate it. Create an opportunity to let His spirit shine through you.

This prosperity requested by David in this Psalm, is translated, *tsaleach*, which has a forceful strength behind it. Tsaleach prosperity is pushed forward; it breaks out and comes mightily. God will clear the way to get your prize to you. And many times, every thing that stands against your blessing is not going to turn to the side and usher in the goods. But God - our powerful, undefeated, in our corner, Savior - is fit to fight. God's prosperity is greater than money in your bank account, clothes in your closet and a car in your garage. You don't want the limited prosperity that man dresses up, sprinkles perfume on, and tries to run by you as genuine. Your desire must be for a different type of success. We know the fleeting nature of the world's success because we see so many with so much and yet so broken on the inside. That void can only be filled with the assurance of knowing you are in a right relationship with your Creator. When that relationship is on point, every other relationship will fall into place. This is not magic potion - what happens is God will speak to you and counsel you on the right decisions you need to make to prosper your relationships with others. Remember, He has your best interest at heart and would love to use you to draw others to Him. We have been used by the world long enough - isn't it time we volunteered to be used by God.

If this is a new way of thinking for you, adjust your mind,

because you will start to see blessings, relationships, and responsibilities in a whole new light.

> If any man be in Christ,
> He is a new creature;
> Old things are passed away;
> Behold, all things are become new.
>
> 2 Corinthians 5:17

As you move through this new dimension of thought, make it a point from this moment on, to stop looking at the natural as your source. Let's talk about some of the characteristics of your true Source. He is Awesome - Living - A Burden Bearer - Eternal - A Mind Fixer - A Heart Regulator - A Solution Creator - A Soul Saver. The greatest news of all is that He has chosen to partner with you. Therefore, this ought to be you relationship with Him:

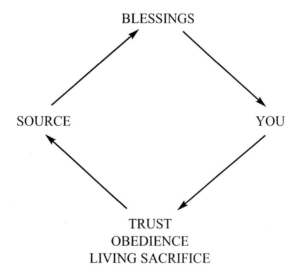

BLESSINGS

SOURCE   YOU

TRUST
OBEDIENCE
LIVING SACRIFICE

Note the cyclical nature of the diagram. Just like any other relationship you have, you know that on some levels, there is a cause and effect factor. When you do a, b, and c, then you can expect d, e, and f. This relationship is no different in many ways. Examine some of the If... Then scenarios God points out in His Word:

> If my people, which are called by my name,
> shall humble themselves, and pray,
> and seek my face, and turn from their
> wicked ways; then will I hear from heaven,
> and will forgive their sin, and will heal their land.
> 2 Chronicles 7:14

> If ye will obey my voice indeed,
> and keep my covenant,
> then you shall be a peculiar treasure
> unto me above all people:
> for all the earth is mine.
> Exodus 19:5

> If from thence thou shalt seek the
> Lord thy God, thou shalt find Him,
> If thy seek Him with all thy heart
> and with all thy soul.
> Deuteronomy 4:29

"If... Then" scenarios are so powerful because they leave no room for misinterpretation. God will stand by His word and He wants you to exercise the same type of integrity. God is just and He is a God of balance. Just as He will make your cup overflow with blessings, so also will you pay a hefty price for choosing to disobey Him. Deuteronomy 28:15-68 lists the curses that He can send your way if you choose to turn your back on Him. Suffice it to say, the last thing you want to do is challenge Him.

Be still and know that I am God. (Psalm 46:10). We waste too much time devising, scheming, and plotting our own solutions. If we are still long enough to hear His voice and guidance, then He will do what He does best - provide a tailor made script.

He has knocked on the door, shone the flashlight of truth in our sin, and been gracious enough to open a dialogue. He has even given us the right to remain silent and we don't want to neglect that, knowing that anything we say can be used against us. Our right for a court appointed attorney is gratefully embraced and now, with an absolute leap of faith, we must give Him control. It's almost like the game we played as kids where you stand behind someone and have them lock their knees and fall straight back, into your arms without turning around. That's a picture of complete trust. I have found that the Christian experience is full of many cliches - trust and obey; believe and receive; let go and let God, etc. It is easy to nonchalantly toss these about - even a new Christian will discover the art of interjecting these at the right time. The problem however, is that cliches are not weighty. They are not substantive and will provide a false sense of security.

God's Word, found either in the Bible or whispered into your spirit by your loving Father, is the only thing that will quicken and sustain you. The first step to empowerment and walking in your freedom, is learning His Word. He has bequeathed it to you - He wants you to take ownership of it. Once you own it, you can access it at will, for your own personal use or to share with others.

When the Emancipation Proclamation took effect in January 1863, slaves in Texas were not able to read and because they were residing in a Confederate controlled state, they were not privy to the new law of the land. As a matter of fact, it wasn't until two and a half years later, in June of 1865, that they were made knowledgeable of their freedom. So you see, here is an incredible example of a case where freedom was an unrealized right and because of ignorance, thousands of people continued to suffer. And so it is with many Christians. They have been made free in Christ, and they are still walking around in shackles. They are allowing themselves to be imprisoned by demons of depression, debt, doubt, fear, divisiveness, greed, jealousy, and selfishness, just to name a few. Once you truly recognize your freedom, you then can send old habits packing and make them feel unwanted in your presence. You must invoke your rights - no one else can do it for you. This knowledge is the key to walking in your victory.

It is critical to remember that your rights are not byproducts of any thing that you have done, but rather an outpouring of His righteousness in your behalf. There is a terrific scene in The Lion King movie, where Simba, the main character, is faced with imminent danger. Still being a lion cub, he does not yet carry much clout in the area of terrorizing his opponents. When the hyenas try to attack him, he tries to roar ferociously to protect himself. Of course only his baby voice trickles out, but nevertheless, the adversaries take immediate flight, running for their lives. What Simba didn't realize was that his 400 pound father was standing directly behind him, superimposing his roar over his son's and thereby protecting him with his presence. It is no different with us - we are the mouthpiece and God's Word is the annihilator. Let's look at one of the most acute explanations of the power of His Word:

> The word of God is quick and powerful and
> sharper than any two edged sword, piercing
> even to the dividing asunder of soul and
> spirit and of the joints and marrow, and is
> a discerner of the thoughts and intents of
> the heart.
>
> Hebrews 4:12

One contemporary translation of this scripture can be found in Eugene Peterson's The Message - this is how he phrases the same passage:

> God's powerful word is sharp as a surgeon's
> scalpel, cutting through everything, whether
> doubt or defense, laying us open to listen and

obey. Nothing and no one is impervious to God's Word. We can't get away from it - no matter what.

Now being made aware of the power of His word, you must do an honest inventory of your areas of temptation. Satan's preference is to use your weakness against you. Take note that he didn't tempt Judas with a beautiful woman (see Samson, David) - that area obviously was not a proven weakness. He did aim for his Achilles heel and he won't hesitate to do the same to you. If, before you were saved, your weakness was self-pity or self-hatred, then you need to meditate on scriptures having to do with your new position in Christ, for example:

Romans 3:23;
2 Corinthians 5:17;
and 1 Peter 2:9.

If your weakness was worry or fear, then your meditation must revolve around scriptures like:

Deuteronomy 31:6;
1 Chronicles 19:13;
and Isaiah 41:10.
What about anger - then peace is your meditation - cover yourself with encouragements from:

Psalm 34:14;
Psalm 119:165;
and Psalm 122:7.

Hopefully by now, the pattern is apparent to you - the method is to meditate on the opposite condition. Do not dwell on the problem; dance in the solution and let God make the repairs from the inside out.

You see, we are all a work in progress, and yet the finished product has already been bought with a price. This is a picture of a Divine lay-away purchase. Everything has already been paid for, we are just waiting on the Owner to come by and pick it up. And when He sees us, He shall make an exchange that shall be unprecedented:

> For our conversation is in heaven from
> whence also we look for the Savior, the
> Lord Jesus Christ:
>
> Who shall change our vile body,
> that it may be fashioned like unto
> His glorious body...
>
> Philippians 3:20-21a

We are told in the second chapter of Ephesians that we are His workmanship - we are walking bill boards for Christ. He says that if we will lift Him up in conversation and conduct, then He will draw men to Him. When He knocks, He is presenting us with a second chance; an opportunity to start over from scratch - and here's the best part - with no grudges held against us. We can serve a God who forgives and forgets. We ought to run to the door and swing it open, eager to come out with our hands up, thanking God that the man from Calvary has arrived.

Have You Any Room for Jesus[13]

Have you any room for Jesus,
He who bore your load of sin?
As He knocks and asks admission,
Sinner, will you let Him in?

Room for pleasure, room for business,
But for Christ the Crucified,
Not a place that He can enter,
In the heart for which He died?

Room and time now give to Jesus,
Soon will pass God's day of grace;
Soon thy heart left cold and silent,
And thy Savior's pleading cease.

Room for Jesus, King of glory!
Hasten now His word obey;
Swing the heart's door widely open,
Bid Him enter while you may.

---

1   Corinthians 10:13
2   James 4:4
3   1 Thessalonians 4:7
4   2 Timothy 2:22
5   James 2:12
6   1 Corinthians 13:11
7   Myra Brooks Welch, "Touch of the Master's Hand," The Gospel Messenger, 26 February 1921.
8   Jack W. Hayford, Litt. D., gen. ed. Spirit-Filled Life Bible, p.1342.
    ibid., p. 1704.
10   "Hubble Identifies What May Be Most Luminous Star Known." NASA News, Release #97-133, Oct. 7. 1997.
11   Eugene H. Peterson, The Message, Psalm 130:3-4, p. 724.
12   ibid., p. 465.
13   John R. Rice and Joy Rice Martin, "Have You Any Room for Jesus," Soul-Stirring Songs and Hymns, p.292.

Bibliography for References Cited

Gove, Philip Babcock and Merriam Webster editorial staff. Webster's Third New International Dictionary, Massachusetts: Merriam Webster, inc.

Hayford, Jack W., gen. ed. Spirit-Filled Life Bible, Tennessee: Thomas Nelson Publishers, 1982.

"Hubble Identifies What May Be Most Luminous Star Known." NASA News, Release #97-133; Oct. 7. 1997.

Peterson, Eugene H. The Message, Colorado: Navpress, 1996.

Rice, John R. and Martin, Joy Rice, compilers. "Have You Any Room for Jesus," source unk., arr. by Daniel W. Whittle, Music by CC Williams; Soul-Stirring Songs and Hymns. Tennessee: Sword of the Lord Publishers, 1972.

Ryrie, Charles Caldwell. The Ryrie Study Bible. Chicago: The Moody Bible Institute, 1978.

Strong, James, Strong's Exhaustive Concordance of the Bible. Tennessee: Thomas Nelson Publishers, 1990.

Welch, Myra Brooks. "Touch of the Master's Hand," The Gospel Messenger, Brethren Press, 26 February 1921.

Study Guide for Groups
or Individual Advancement

CHAPTER 1: You Have the Right to Remain Silent

1. Do you have a relationship with God?

There are many terms and phrases people use to identify their standing the the Christian family: born again, saved, believer, washed in the blood, redeemed, and others. The common denominator shared by all of these descriptions, comes down to one word. Relationship.

Do you have a relationship with your Creator? Have you invited Him into your life? There is no time like the present, to seek the Lord. He wants to restore your relationship with Him so He can move to the next level of establishing fellowship. The order of these two events is not optional.

If you do not know Him as your Personal Savior, please obey His leading and say this prayer:

Dear God,

I admit that I am a sinner and I need you to make things right. Please forgive me for my sins and give me a fresh start. I believe you sent your Son, Jesus Christ, to die for my sins - He canceled a debt that I could never pay. Thank you for loving me enough to sacrifice your Son. I want to accept Him into my heart as my Lord and Savior.

Amen

2. You may already be saved, but have you surrendered?

Are you still playing tug of war with God in certain areas where He should have complete control? Identify one area where you need to release your control and let Him rule. For the next week, purpose in your heart to turn a specific area completely over to Him. Let Him be God.

3. Do you talk too much?

We are in a super charged world, where estimations are measured in milliseconds. Events are happening so speedily, that yesterday's front page is tomorrow's ancient history. To keep up with that pace, we do a lot of communicating - fax machines, emails, instant messaging, cell phones, pagers, etc. Are you taking time to commune with the One who gave you the voice to talk? Let's examine how Merriam-Webster's Dictionary defines 'commune':

    a. to hold converse or intercommunication, especially with great mental or spiritual depth or intensity;
    b. to attain an earnest or deep feeling of unity, appreciation, and receptivity.

When you walk away from your time with God, do you feel refreshed? In spending quality time with Him, you should sense a time of exchange - you are giving Him your weakness and He is giving you His strength. If you are talking too much, then maybe you are completing only the first part of the equation. If you are feeling lightened, but not empowered, then focus on less talking and more listening to the Great Counselor.

4. Are you meeting your potential in the "small areas"?

Are you punctual, supportive, kind, and forgiving? We can use these examples just as a starting point. If you are faithful in small areas such as these, then stretching out to larger areas will be a natural growth process for you. You will not fear moving to the next level, because as you stay focused on increased opportunities to bless others, God will side swipe you with blessings, greater responsibilities, and insights on fulfilling your potential.

5. Silence is golden - what does that really mean?

That may be an appropriate idiom to describe an escape from the cacophony of our busy world, but silence does not matter in our confessions to God. He hears our heart the loudest because He knows our motives. In seeking forgiveness, do you approach Him with excuses and rationalizations or do you take responsibility for your wrong choices which led you to wrong actions? What is the difference between sins of omission versus commission?

CHAPTER 2: Anything You Say Can Be Used Against You

1. How do you use your mouth?

What kind of conversations do you have with other people? Are you constantly complaining and pointing out the shortcomings of those in your circle? Do you encourage others and speak well of them even in their absence? On the road to success, is your mouth a stepping stone or a stumbling block? Make a conscious effort to sincerely complement three people every day, for the next week. Use your mouth to bless, not to curse.

2. Who has rulership over you - your Flesh, Satan, or your Spirit?

Remember that attacks made by your flesh or Satan, have the goal of killing you - all at one time, or little by little. Things that tear down, diminish or mock your values or your spirit, are typically not of God. Yes, spiritual growth initiated by the Spirit of God, can break you down - but it won't take you down. The purpose of God's approach is to humble you and build you back up, based on His principles. His methods deal with replacement therapy - removing you and putting Himself in your place. When your spirit communes on a regular basis with God's Spirit, then harmony is established and you will seek and desire the same things for yourself that He does. Take time to focus on your actions and refuse to operate in an automatic pilot mode, where you are not aware of the conception of your decisions. Make an accounting of how often you were just going to think, speak, or act a certain way, just because that was your natural tendency. How many times can you catch yourself?

3. What are you famous for?

What sin, either recently or in the past, has proven to be your downfall? Lust? Greed? Jealousy? Laziness? What specific scriptures can you find to help you combat this weakness? Use a Bible Concordance to help you locate the antidotes. Write them down on paper and meditate on them daily until they take root in your heart.

4. Can you do all things?

Do you believe in yourself? Do you encourage yourself or do you spend more time in the neighborhood of self-destruction? What inner talks do you have with yourself? Forget about your 3 year, 5 year, and 10 plans, just for a moment. What can you do to make today more successful? What can you say to yourself to turn the next corner? Every time you recognize a problem today, whether with yourself or your circumstances, come up with three possible solutions. Lives can be changed just by the power of one individual who decides there is a better way.

5. What do you dwell on?

True, noble, pure, honorable thoughts - with these kinds of seeds, what type of harvest could you expect? Are you one to let worry creep into your space? Do you constantly fret and frustrate yourself when it comes to challenges in your life? If you dwell near the surface, not far from the sunlight and oxygen, you will set yourself up for growth and fruitfulness. However, dwelling near the bottom, leads to a scavenger outlook, and you end up meditating on thoughts that just decay in your spirit and lead to ill emotional and psychological health. Put a "thought colander" into your mind that will serve as a force to keep negative thoughts at bay, We know they will still come your way, but the more you practice the art of selective thinking, the less attention these negative thoughts will demand. Pay attention to negative conversations in your presence. Refuse to take part in them because the words thrown around aimlessly in the break room, will try to take root in your spirit and nullify the positive strides you are making. Avoid negativity like it is a curse and watch your spirit soar.

CHAPTER 3: You Have the Right to an Attorney

1. Who would you die for?

I would venture to say that most of us would die for maybe a handful of people - and they would have to be very close relatives or friends. Would you die for someone who denied your importance in their life? What about for someone who didn't even like you? Think of someone from your past who hurt you and imagine yourself stepping between them and harm's way. Imagine the type of unconditional love you would have to have to act in this manner. This is the type of love that God has for you - how magnificent it is for someone to voluntarily take your death sentence. Either a) you must be very special; b) there must be a special mission in store for you; or c) all of the above. For today, marvel on God's love for you and thank Him for making the ultimate sacrifice. Adopt a spirit of not wanting to disappoint Him.

2. What is your most shining moment?

Think back over the last ten years and pick out your greatest accomplishment. Recall the hard work, training, and effort that went into obtaining the victory. Remember all the onlookers and supporting friends who cheered you on and offered enthusiastic congratulations. Now imagine if God had not been in the picture. What if He determined that He was not going to allow you to succeed - could you have gone around Him and appealed to a higher authority? God has His hand in every good thing that happens to you. You win when He says you can win and not a moment before. Before we polish the trophies and cash the bonus checks, let's remember to thank Him for the awards and the opportunities. Be sure to thank God for all that He allows to come your way as well as for all the harmful things that He keeps from you. Trust in His timing and remember that Father really does know best.

3. Have you been completely truthful today?

What exactly is a little white lie? Some would say it is but a small avoidance of the whole truth and it does not really hurt anyone. Truthfully speaking, any utterance spoken by you that chips away at your integrity or character, is indeed harmful to you. Like a small crack in your car's windshield, first it is barely noticeable. But then the little lies can grow or multiply and spider web into compromises on many other levels. When we are completely honest, we are not giving the enemy ammunition to use against us at a later time. Be 100% honest today - and if you are put in a position where a person's feelings may be at stake, just remember to season the truth with love.

4. Are you out of tune?

The Master wants to prune you and use you. Are you readying yourself? Have you been in training so that when it's time to get on the field, you can hit the ground running? Are you fit to fight or are you approaching life as though it were off season? What is your mission? What seeds were planted in you, even at your conception, waiting to burst beyond their covering. Who (besides yourself) are you shortchanging, by not walking in your purpose?

List five things that you are good at, particularly in the area of blessing others. Here are a few examples - teaching, encouraging, helping, exercising compassion. Remember, there may not be a direct, obvious connection, e.g. you may not work in a nursing home but you receive great satisfaction in caring for and visiting with the elderly. This natural drawing in your spirit may be a manifestation of the gift of encouragement - wow - isn't that a critical gift for the body of Christ. If you are not exercising your gift on purpose, commit some serious time and prayer to asking God for direction. Your gift is actually for the benefit of His kingdom. Do you think He wants you to spend one more day not doing what He designed you to do?

CHAPTER 4: Released on Your Own Recognizance

1. How do others recognize you?

How well do people really know you? Are there behaviors that you exhibit when no one else is around - or at least no one in authority over you? How would ten of your acquaintances describe you? What about three of your best friends? Would there be any overlap in their testimonies? Are you consistent in your character or do you put on different faces for different audiences? I'm not talking about the obvious professional versus parental, but rather the compassionate listener versus the town crier. Your consistent character, led by integrity, will set an example for others. List ten adjectives that others would use to describe you. Then list ten self-describing adjectives - are there any matches?

2. The truth shall set you free.

What does that statement mean to you? What is the difference between knowing the truth and applying the truth? How has a particular revelation of a truth (Biblical or non-Biblical) blessed you?

3. Are you patient in your relationship with God?

If God doesn't answer you immediately, does discouragement quickly set in? Do you habitually try to put Him on your time table? What methods do you implement while you await His response? When He answers your prayer and says 'no', are you a pouter or a truster? Recall one event in your past where you desired Plan A and he prescribed Plan B, which in hindsight turned out to be the better Plan. Be sure to visit this occasion the next time He says 'no'.

4. Has God ever used your enemy to bless you?

God is the Chief Orchestrater - nothing happens without His permission; He is never surprised. Not only is He going to make His enemies bow down to Him, at His set time, but He also makes our enemies bless us. This reminds us of His sovereignty. What circumstances seemed to be mounting against you when God stepped up and turned the tables?

5. Where is your faith?

Is your faith embryonic, adolescent, or fully matured? What are you feeding it? Are you exercising it and letting it out to get fresh air? Are you walking by faith or by fear? Increasing your faith takes a concerted effort and demands attention. Concentrate on ways to build your faith into great faith that trusts God and agrees with His handling of your situation. Pray to God, every day, to increase your faith.

Ordering Information

There are 2 easy options to order additional copies of Come Out with Your Hands Up:

** Send a money order along with this completed form or duplicate infomation to:

Success in the Mirror
ATTN: Kimberley McDaniel
P.O. Box 39366
Baltimore, Md. 21212

Make Payable to: Success in the Mirror

Name _____

Address _____

_____

Daytime Phone Number _____

Quantity of books (x $12.00 each) _____

Subtotal _____

MD residents add
5% sales tax _____

Shipping: $4.00 or 7% (whichever is greater)

_____

Total enclosed _____

** For quantity discounts, see chart on following page. [And then we lead into the quantity discount info that follows]

Quantity Discounts

10 - 24 books	$11.00 each
25 - 49 books	$10.00 each
50 - 99 books	$9.00 each
100 - 249 books	$8.00 each

For Quantities greater than 250,
contact my office directly at 410.433.7411.

**Alternate ordering options can be found on line at:
www.successinthemirror.com

Be sure to check out the articles and follow the online
ordering instructions.